# Introduction

G000240595

This book introduces our new range of moulds. We have developed an original concept in mould production. I myself to ensure that the finished item looks handmade. The principal behind this is to enable novices to pro inspire them to want to learn more about the art of sugarcraft. In addition for the experienced or professional obtained greatly reducing time and costs. The moulds are produced from the highest quality silicone available and will not rip or tear Please follow the instructions on page 33 on how to use the moulds.

Magic Sparkles have been used on the cakes in this book. They are edible and safe to use on any cake decorating from fairy cakes to wedding cakes. They can be used on cakes, sweets, chocolates or desserts for a special touch.
Use straight from the pot or grind down to a finer glitter. To do this, either leave in the pot and stir with a teaspoon handle or use a pestle and mortar. To attach to cakes the surface should be tacky not wet - if too wet they will dissolve. Edible glue - see recipe below, is ideal although you can use water or alcohol. Their appearance is enhanced by good lighting - halogen or spotlights work well.

### How To Use The Size Guide (CC)

On any instructions for modelling in this book I have used the Cel Cakes Size Guide. This should make it easier to produce proportioned figures. To achieve the correct size, the ball of paste should sit in the correct hole (size below it) with 1/3 of the paste showing out of the bottom and 2/3 out of the top (this does not apply to the smallest sizes). You will then have approximately the correct size ball of paste to shape.

# Recipes

| Modelling Paste | Mexican Paste | Royal Icing | Softened Sugarpaste | Edible Glue | Edible Supports |
|---|---|---|---|---|---|
| Either:- $^1/_2$ sugarpaste, $^1/_2$ flower paste kneaded together, or knead 5ml (1tsp) of gum tragacanth into 225g (8ozs) sugarpaste and leave for 8 hours, or knead 5ml (1tsp) Tylo (CMC) powder into 225g (8ozs) sugarpaste. | Mix together 225g (8ozs) of icing sugar and 3 level teaspoons of gum tragacanth. Add 25ml (5tsp) of cold water (taken from tap). Mix together, turnout and knead well. Store in a plastic bag and a sealed container for 6-8 hours to mature. The paste will feel very hard but will soften up easily. Break off small pieces and soften in your fingers. Matured paste will freeze. | Place 30ml (6 level tsp) of merriwhite in a mixing bowl and gradually add 5tbs cold water mixing with a wooden spoon until free from lumps. Add 225g (8ozs) of icing sugar and mix until smooth. Add 110g (4ozs) of icing sugar and then add the rest gradually until the correct consistency is reached. Beat well for approximately 5 minutes. Store in the fridge, in an airtight container. It should keep for 4 weeks. | Place the amount of sugarpaste you want to soften in a bowl. Chop up roughly and then gradually add drops of cold water. Break down with a fork or a spoon and mix until smooth and lump free. Continue until required consistency is reached. The first time you do this, be careful not to add too much water too soon. It softens quickly. | This is easily made with 1 part Tylo (CMC) powder to 25-30 parts water. Place the powder in a bottle or jar that has a lid. Add the water, replace the lid and shake. There will be thick creamy white pieces in the water. They will dissolve and the liquid will become clear by the following day. | (for modelled figures). These are easily made from any left over Mexican paste. Roll out long thin sausage pieces and cut different lengths. Leave to dry for at least six hours. When used in modelled figures they are a safe alternative to cocktail sticks etc. |

**NOTE:** ANY SPECIAL EQUIPMENT USED HAS A SUPPLIER CODE. FOR EXAMPLE – SIZE GUIDE (CC) – SUPPLIER CEL CAKES.
SEE ACKNOWLEDGMENTS PAGE 37 .

# Ballerinas

20cm (8in) hexagonal cake (measured side to side) marzipanned and iced placed on a 33cm (13in) iced cake drum board, 560g modelling paste, royal icing, 1 pot of white magic sparkles ground finer (p1), edible glue (p1), isopropyl alcohol.

Paste Colours: Grape violet, pink, ice blue, paprika, cream and hair colours (SF).

Powder colours: Black, white, pink (SC), snowflake lustre (SK).

Small face mould (Karen Davies), garrett frill cutter (PME), blossom cutter (PME), bow cutter size 2 (JEM), veining / frilling stick / mouth tool (JEM), size guide (p1) (CC), 40cm of 38mm wide wired ribbon for each skirt, 6cm circle cutter, no.1 & no.42 piping nozzles, small flower stamens, a selection of dusting and paint brushes, florist tape light green, 2 pieces of white wire between sizes 26 – 30, greaseproof paper, a piece of spaghetti.

1 Cut a strip of paper 8cm wide to fit around cake sides adding 2cm to length. Fold back 2cm, then fold into 6 equal sections. Hold against the side of your cake and mark where the top of the garrett frill will be and the centre. Fold along the centre and draw a curve up to the top point. Keep folded then cut along the drawn curve. Open out the template and place around the cake. Make sure it is in the correct position, before pinning into position with a cocktail stick where the ends overlap. Mark the curved line onto each side of the cake with a knife or a cocktail stick. Remove pattern. Soften a little sugarpaste or use royal icing to pipe a small plain shell using a no.1 nozzle around base of cake.

2 Colour 3 pieces of modelling paste (each 70g) in pink, lilac and blue. Roll out one colour and cut out a garrett frill. Cut open then check length of frill against cake and trim to fit. Frill around edge with the veining tool. Prevent from sticking to work surface with a little icing sugar. Brush a line of glue 3mm below marked line on cake. Attach frill. Keep each end of frill below the marked line. Repeat with the next colour overlapping the previous frill when attaching. When the 6 coloured pieces are attached, add a layer in the cake colour. Pipe a small plain shell where frill attaches to cake.

3 Roll out coloured modelling paste and cut out 2 bows in each colour. Dust with snowflake lustre. First attach tails over the point of each garrett frill, then the bow over, folding the loops into the centre, followed by the knot over the loop joins.

4 Colour a little modelling paste ivory. Roll out, dust with snowflake lustre then cut out blossoms. You will need 16 small, 12 medium and 6 large. Brush centres thinly with glue and insert a stamen pushing the flower up until secure. Leave to dry. Cut each piece of ribbon into half. Hold one end of a wire securely and gather up from opposite end. Tie the two ends together and trim.

5 Colour 255g modelling paste with pink and paprika for the skin colour (brown can be added to this for darker skin). For each leg measure a size 11 ball of paste on the size guide. Roll out to 90cm, keeping narrower for the foot. Cut a small edge off the end of the foot and add a small teardrop in coloured paste for the shoe. Dust with snowflake lustre. Press two legs together at the top, put into a sitting position on the cake. Bend both outwards then cross over. Roll out coloured paste and cut out 2 skirts for each ballerina using the circle cutter. Dust with snowflake then frill with the veining tool and attach over legs.

6 from size 12 balls of skin coloured paste pulling up a little for neck. Roll out coloured paste and cut a strip 9 x 5cm. Dust with snowflake lustre then turn over. Cut out a neck in centre of one long side. Place body front side down onto coloured paste. Wrap one side up to back to see where to trim then repeat with other side – they should overlap slightly. Turn over then trim through all paste to get a straight waist. Push a piece of spaghetti through body and up out of neck. Place ribbon skirts on to body, then position the body on top of skirt and push spaghetti through legs. Break off spaghetti leaving 3cm showing above neck. Pinch the neck up the spaghetti.

7 Brush glue thinly onto blossoms and six stamens. Sprinkle with magic sparkles. Cut wires into 7cm lengths. Using half width stretched florist tape attach a stamen, then a small blossom, 2 medium and one large to a piece of wire. You will need 2 for each ballerina.

8 Arms are each shaped from size 9 balls of paste. Mark fingers with a knife. Attach one arm, check length of flower stem and trim if necessary. Twist 2 stems together and lay over arm. Attach other arm over securing the flowers. Colour a little royal icing in each colour. Place in a piping bag and trim point to the size of a no.1 nozzle. Pipe a wavy line around neck of bodice.

9 Using the largest size on the face mould, make 3 full heads (see page 30). Press ears back. Dust cheeks with a little pink powder. Paint eyes with white powder mixed with isopropyl alcohol. Paint in the black so each will be looking in the appropriate direction. Add a tiny white dot to each eye. Paint eyebrows and eyelashes using a fine paintbrush and colour mixed with water. Trim necks off heads. Brush top of neck on body with a little glue. Attach heads. Position so they are slightly turned or at an angle.

10 Colour royal icing for hair and pipe using a no.42 nozzle. Trim stems off back of blossoms and push into hair.

# Cat Birthday Cake

20cm (8in) cake iced in lilac coloured sugarpaste, 30cm (12in) cake board, sugarpaste, modelling paste, royal icing, isopropyl alcohol, edible glue, trex.

Paste Colours: : Ice blue, pink, egg yellow, spruce green, black (SF).

Powder Colours: silver, bronze, snowflake lustre (SK), white, black, pink (SC).

Cat mould (Karen Davies), basket mould (Karen Davies), bow cutter from confetti set (PC), embosser (HP), clay gun (optional), no.1 piping nozzle, beads on a string – approximately 84cm, non stick rolling board, a selection of dusting and paint brushes.

**1** Place cake on board. Ice board and emboss edge. Attach beads with royal icing.

**2** Use the basket mould and modelling paste to make basket base. Leave to dry.

**3** Colour small pieces of modelling paste in pink, blue and yellow. Add some yellow colour to the green paste to get the lime shade. Mould a ball of wool in each colour. Roll out each colour of paste and cut out a shape for the knitting. The top of the knitting should be shaped to fit under the knitting needles. Attach to sides of cake using glue.

**4** Colour some modelling paste grey. Soften with trex if using the clay gun. Either roll 10 very thin sausages 4-5cm long or use a clay gun to make the knitting needles. Point each at one end. Attach to sides of cake above knitting, points together. Keep one pair to put in basket.

**5** Colour a little royal icing grey and pipe lettering on cake. Leave to dry then paint with silver powder mixed with isopropyl alcohol. Paint knitting needles.

**6** Use white modelling paste in the mould to make the cat. Dust pink powder into ears. Paint the eyes and nose black. Add a tiny white highlight to the eyes. Attach cat to cake. Soften some sugarpaste with water. Place a little in a piping bag then colour the rest black. Pipe the softened paste onto the cat. Do the ears and tail

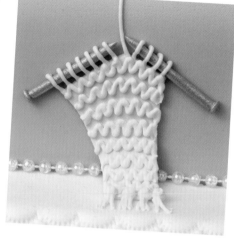

tip first spreading icing with a damp paintbrush. Dab at it to get the fur effect. Swap to the black but leave the face and top of chest for the white. Pipe a few little tufts of hair on top of the head. Finish with a little white around face and on chest. Grease a rolling out board and the bow cutter with trex. Roll out white Mexican paste and cut out a bow. Remove bow from board and dust with pink powder followed by snowflake lustre. Attach to cat.

**7** Use the basket mould and modelling paste to make basket side. Dust both pieces of basket with bronze powder. Pipe a little icing under cats paws and attach basket base. Attach basket side. Position the balls of wool and needles then attach. Colour a little royal icing in each wool colour. Pipe stitches over the needles. Pipe squiggly lines over each piece of knitting. From the top centre of each knitted piece, pipe a line up to the top of the cake towards the cat in the basket. Pipe a few over the cat and then take each one to their ball of wool finishing with a few lines over each.

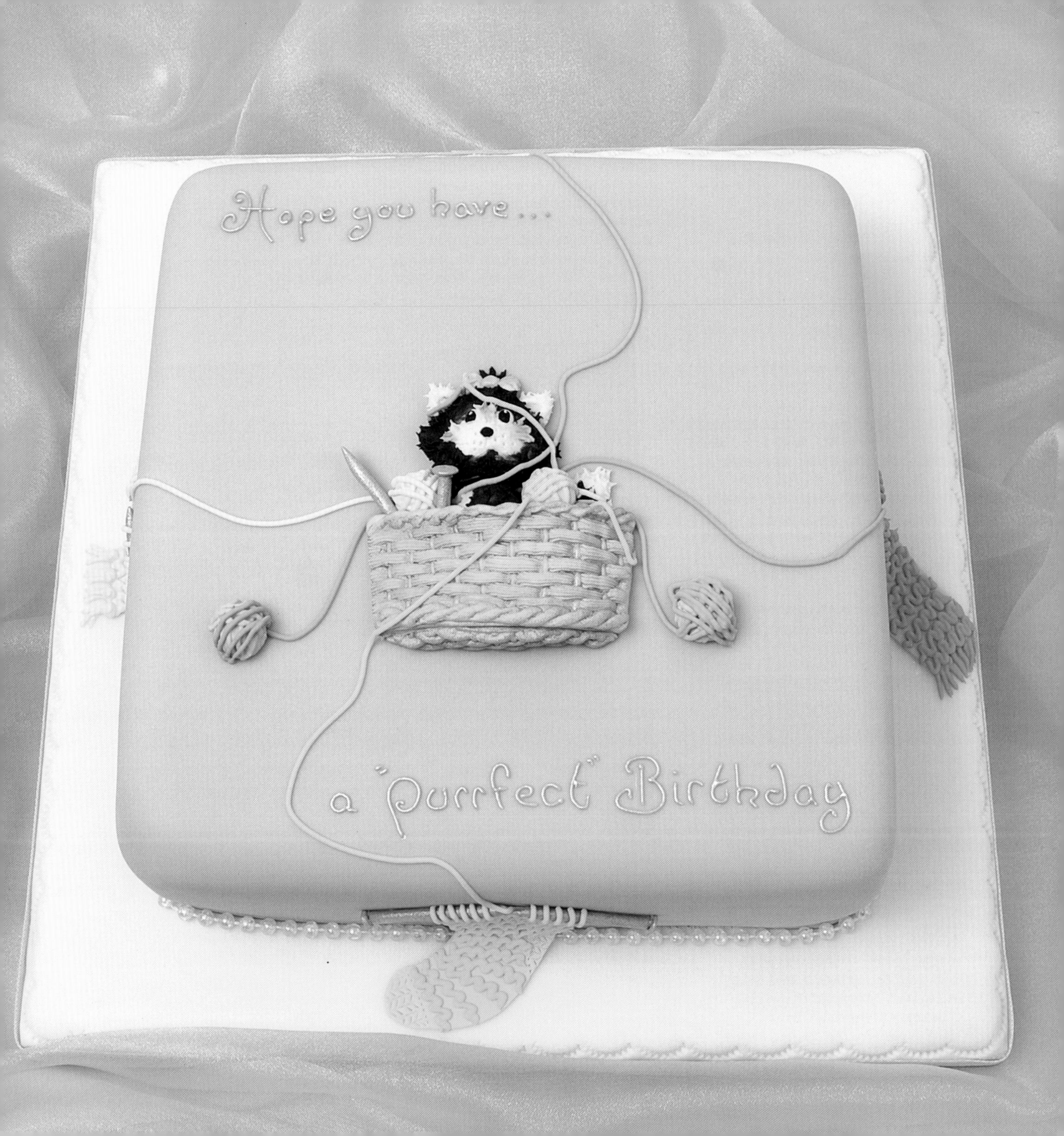
Hope you have...
a "purrfect" Birthday

# Baby and Toys

20cm (8in) cake, 28cm (11in) board, 1kg sugarpaste, modelling paste, small piece of marzipan, royal icing, edible glue.

Paste Colours: Pink, grape violet, dark brown, black, paprika (SF).

Powder colours: Pink, white, black, blue, (SC), snowflake lustre (SK).
Spray colour: pearl (PME).

Teddy mould, duck mould, rabbit mould, small face mould (Karen Davies), stork and small teddy from make a cradle set (PC), nappy pin, bottle and rattle from lion nursery set (PC), size guide (CC), no.42 & no.3 piping nozzles, bow cutter (FMM), stitch wheel / dresden tool (PME), 2cm circle cutter, selection of dusting and painting brushes.

1 Place cake on board. Ice cake and emboss with teddy, stork, bottle, rattle and nappy pin. Ice around board edge. Soften some sugarpaste (p1) and colour pink. Place in a piping bag with a no.42 nozzle and pipe small shells around base of cake. Spray cake and board with pearl lustre.

2 Colour 3 pieces of modelling paste in very pale shades of pink, lilac and brown. Use to mould 3 each of the teddy, duck and rabbit. Use pink powder to dust in teddy's ears, paws and cheeks, the duck's feet and beak, the rabbit's nose, paws and under ears. Brush over all toys with snowflake lustre. Dip a cocktail stick into black paste colour and mark a small dot into each eye. Attach to sides of cake with royal icing.

3 Make the baby as on page 8, but use the following sizes from the size guide: body 15, legs each 11, (make and attach the teddy bear parts once legs are attached to baby – see instruction 4), hands each 4, arms each 8, head middle size on small face mould. Use a 2cm circle cutter for the collar.

4 Shape a small teddy from marzipan coloured with a little brown paste colour. First shape and attach small legs and feet. Next attach an arm to the baby's body. Shape and attach the teddy's body marking the centre with a stitch line then attach the other arm. Roll a small ball and attach for head. Attach a snout and emboss a mouth with a no.3 piping nozzle. Add tiny ears. Mark eyes with a cocktail stick and black paste colour. Roll a tiny ball for the nose and attach. Paint black with paste colour mixed with water.

5 Attach baby to cake with softened sugarpaste.

# Teddy, Duck and Rabbit

15cm (6in) cake iced in chosen colour and placed on 20cm (8in) board, modelling paste, sugarpaste, marzipan, 2 pots of magic sparkles in colour to match cake, an edible support 4cm long (p1), isopropyl alcohol, edible glue (p1).

Paste Colours: Colours of your choice but could include, pink, egg yellow, ice blue, baby blue, peach, brown; black (SF).

Powder Colours: Pink, white, black, eye colour of choice (SC), snowflake lustre (SK).

Teddy mould, duck mould, or rabbit mould small face mould, baby & teddy mould (for the teddy the babies are holding) (Karen Davies), stork and small teddy embossers from the make a cradle set (PC), stitch wheel/dresden tool (PME), button stick (HP), bow cutter (FMM), frilling/veining/mouth tool (JEM), 3cm circle cutter, size guide (CC), an embosser or crimper for edge of icing on board, assorted dusting and paintbrushes, scissors.

1 Colour modelling paste in the colours you require for the teddies, ducks or rabbits. Measure around your cake and calculate how many toys you will need. Mould the required number of figures you require (approximately 12 for this size cake). Dust pink into rabbit and teddies ears, their paws and cheeks. Dust the ducks beak and feet. Dust figures with snowflake lustre. Dip the tip of a cocktail stick into black paste colour and mark eyes. Paint noses on rabbits and teddies using black powder colour mixed with isopropyl alcohol. Leave to dry.

2 Grind the two pots of magic sparkles finer (p1). Spread edible glue (it should be quite a thin consistency so add water if needed) over top of cake using a large brush. Work it over the sides to the bottom of the cake. Sprinkle the sparkles over the top of the cake tilting to remove excess. Tilt the cake and apply some sparkles to the sides. Work it around the sides gradually starting at the top. If there isn't enough to finish down to the cake board it doesn't matter because the figures will hide this.
Ice the cake board and either emboss or crimp around the edge. Attach the figures with softened sugarpaste.

3 Using the size guide measure 2 size 16 balls of modelling paste and a size 12. Add the 3 pieces together and colour for baby's suit.

With the marzipan measure a size 15 ball plus some extra for hands. Colour with a little pink and peach to get the skin colour.

4 For the baby's body measure a size 16 and 14. Knead together and roll into a smooth ball. Make pear shaped and attach to cake. Push chest back slightly so baby has a tummy. Mark up front with the stitch wheel. Add tiny balls of paste for buttons and emboss with the button stick. Emboss suit with a teddy or stork. Shape legs each from a size 13 ball of paste. Roll a sausage wider at one end. Near the narrow end, roll your little finger across to make the ankle. Bend foot up, flatten a little then pinch at back for heel. Bend slightly at the knee and mark creases at the back with a dresden tool. Brush side of body with glue, narrow leg slightly at top and attach to body.

5 Make a teddy from the baby and teddy mould out of marzipan. Dust with pink powder into ears and onto cheeks and paws. Dust brown powder around.

25cm (10in) iced petal shaped cake, 30cm (12in) round cake drum, block of sugarpaste cut to measure 10 x 7.5 x 2.2cm (sides must be straight), 250g sugarpaste, mexican paste, modelling paste, small piece of marzipan, edible glue (p1), trex.

Paste Colours: Ice blue, peach, pink (SF).

Powder Colours: Snowflake lustre, pink, blue, brown, white, black.

Baby & Teddy mould (Karen Davies), teddy cutters from make a cradle set (PC), bow cutter size 2 (Jem) strip cutter size 3 (JEM), veining/mouth embossing tool (JEM), stitch wheel (PME), garrett frill cutter, no.1 piping nozzle, piece of cake dowelling, a size 18 white wire, white florist tape, non stick rolling out board, assorted painting & dusting brushes, sponge pad.

1. Place cake on board. Colour some sugarpaste pale blue and ice board. Emboss with small teddy then brush with snowflake lustre.

2. Roll out Mexican paste and cut out back for cot (see pattern p36). Grease a non stick board with trex and roll out Mexican paste. Use the strip cutter to cut out 25 strips (plus a few spares). Trim to measure 8cm then place strips and cot back on a sponge pad to dry keeping straight and flat. When dry, dust all with snowflake lustre.

3. Soften a little sugarpaste with water (p1) and colour peach. Place in a piping bag with a no.1 nozzle and pipe a small plain shell around base of cake.

4. Dust mould with a little cornflour. Roll a small oval of white modelling paste smooth and press into teddy mould. Release then dust pink powder into ears, onto paws and cheeks. Dust blue powder around edge, over seams and joins on teddy, then all over with snowflake lustre. Cut half way up where legs join body then bend to sit up. Attach to cake. Mix isopropyl alcohol with

black and white powder and paint a grey nose. You will need 7 bears.

5. Colour the marzipan with a little peach and pink paste colour for skin. Colour 30g of modelling paste pale blue. Roll 2 tiny balls of marzipan and press into baby's hands. Brush a little glue very thinly onto the back of hands. Place modelling paste into mould and press firmly up to neck. Remove body then cut one arm so it will move away from body and attach a teddy under using glue. Place marzipan into head, press and remove. Paint buttons and collar white. Brush cheeks with a little pink powder. Mix brown powder colour with a little water and paint eyebrows, a fine line along lower eyelid, then eyelashes. Attach body then head to block of sugarpaste (cot base). Colour a little royal icing brown and pipe baby's hair. Attach the cot base to the cake.

6. Colour a piece of modelling paste peach. Roll out a small piece of Mexican paste on trex and cut out a 5cm square. Use the strip cutter to cut out a strip of peach paste to attach to top edge of square to make a blanket. Use the stitch wheel along the edge then dust with snowflake

lustre. Crumple up slightly then attach over baby's legs making sure that it doesn't go over the edge of the block.

7. Grease non stick rolling board and large teddy cutter with trex. Roll out white Mexican paste and cut out teddy. Dust with pink, blue and snowflake powders to match moulded teddies. Paint eyes and nose then attach to the centre of the back piece of cot. Attach to back of sugarpaste block with royal icing. Attach bars of cot spacing evenly. Leave to dry.

8. Roll out peach modelling paste thinly and cut out garrett frills. Dust with snowflake lustre, cut open circle then frill using the veining tool. Use glue to attach around cot base. Repeat using white paste but add a line of stitching. Attach a little higher to show peach frill.

9. Cut out more strips using modelling paste, Use a little glue to attach strips over top edges of cot bars. Pinch to secure. Leave to dry then dust with snowflake.

10. Fold wire in half. Now fold 5cm from one end but to 90 degrees. Tape the long part of the wire to dowelling with top of dowelling at bend in wire. Push the dowelling into the cake behind the back of cot leaving a length of 14cm showing. Colour some modelling paste pale blue. Working quickly, roll the paste out thinly on trex. Cut to measure 23 x 14cm. Keep a 23cm edge straight for the top. Round off the 2 bottom corners. Emboss with the small teddy. Frill down sides and along bottom edge. Mark edge of frill with the stitch wheel. Gather the straight edge together then press to secure with a small rolling pin. Pipe royal icing along wire over cot, along top side edges of back of cot and on the edge over 3 bars on each side. Fold gathered edge of drape in half and press over wire. Leave to dry, supporting with kitchen paper or wadding if needed. When dry attach a strip of peach paste along both sides of the top edge of drape. Cut out the bow pieces, dust and attach with royal icing.

20cm (8in) cake marzipanned and iced in ivory sugarpaste, 275g ivory sugarpaste, modelling paste, a little natural marzipan coloured with a little pink and peach (add brown for a darker skin colour), a little royal icing, 3 pots of hint of lemon magic sparkles ground finer (p1), isopropyl alcohol, edible glue.

Paste Colours: **Pink, ice blue, a colour for hair (SF).**

Powder Colours: **Pink, blue, white, eye colour, black, colours for toys (SC), snowflake lustre, gold (SK).**

Spray colour: **Pearl (PME).**

Mitten mould, bootie mould, nursery border, small faces mould (Karen Davies), bow cutter (FMM), no.1 piping nozzle.

**1** Place cake on board. Spray cake all over with snowflake lustre. Clean spray off cake board then cover with sugarpase. Use a large brush to apply glue thinly over iced board. Cover board with magic sparkles.

**2** Using the no.1 nozzle and royal icing, pipe lettering onto cake. Mix isopropyl alcohol with gold powder and paint lettering.

**3** Colour 20g of modelling paste pink and 25g blue. Press into moulds for the mitten and the bootie. Release then dust ribbons and bows with pink and blue powder. Dust all over both with snowflake lustre. Attach to top of cake with glue.

**4** Roll 4 small balls of marzipan for hands. Shape each to a teardrop shape and mark tiny fingers with a knife. Brush a little glue underneath and attach them over the tops of the mitten and bootie leaving enough room for the heads. Press marzipan into the second smallest face on the mould (flat at back) then release. Make 2 faces. Dust cheeks with pink powder. Mix isopropyl alcohol with white powder and paint eyes. Paint the colour into the eye so the babies will be looking at each other. Paint in black pupils then a tiny white highlight. Mix brown powder with water this time and use a very fine brush to paint eyebrows and eyelashes.

**5** Mix a little royal icing for the hair colour and pipe onto heads. Cut out a bow in white modelling paste. Trim off ribbon tails then dust with pink powder followed by snowflake. Attach to girls hair. Make a dummy from modelling paste. Flatten a small ball of paste and attach over mouth with glue. Make a hole in the centre with a cocktail stick. Rub a little trex into the palm of your hand then roll a very thin sausage. Bring the two ends together and press. Lift up on the cocktail stick and paint a little glue onto the end. Push into hole in centre of circle.

**6** Press white modelling paste into the nursery border mould. It is usually easier to make the border one half at a time because it is quite long. Release from mould and dust with desired colours before finishing with snowflake lustre. Dot eyes with a cocktail stick dipped in black paste colour. Attach to cake.

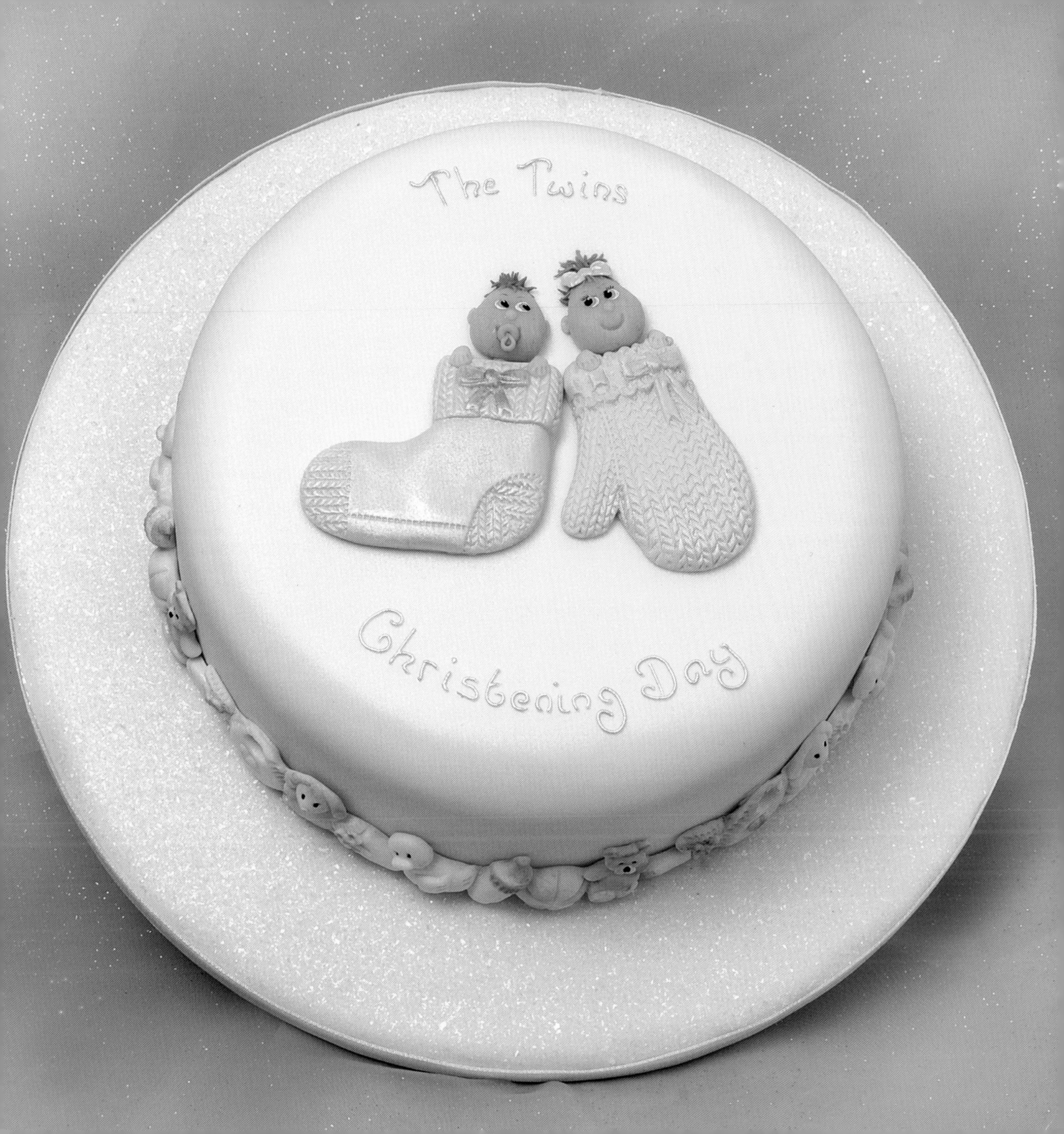
The Twins
Christening Day

# Cosy Christmas

20cm (8in) cake marzipanned and iced placed on a 33cm (13in) cake drum, 350g sugarpaste, modelling paste, 3 pots of white magic sparkles ground finer (p1), isopropyl alcohol, a little royal icing, edible glue (p1).

Paste Colours: Ice blue, black (SF).

Powder Colours: Pink (SC), snowflake lustre, silver (SK).

Spray Colour: Baby blue, pearl (PME).

Mitten mould, teddy mould (Karen Davies), small snowflake plunger cutter (PME), no.1 piping nozzle, dresden tool, assorted dusting and paint brushes,

1 Shake spray can then spray the blue randomly over cake. Finish with the pearl. Clean colour off cakeboard then cover with sugarpaste. Use a large brush to brush glue thinly all over board. Cover with sparkles. Colour a little royal icing grey then using a no.1 nozzle, pipe a small plain shell around base of cake. Pipe lettering on top of cake. Mix silver powder colour with isopropyl alcohol and paint shells and lettering. Colour 50g of modelling paste blue. Keep 5g back for the hats. Press modelling paste well into the mitten and bootie moulds then turn out. Trim away the ribbon tails on the mitten up to the wrist. Smooth area then use a dresden tool

to mark to match knitted pattern. Carefully smooth down the bows on the mitten and bootie. Brush across top area with a little glue. Roll out white sugarpaste and cut 2 oblongs measuring 6 x 2.5cm. Attach to top of mitten and bootie. Brush thinly with glue and cover with sparkles.

2 Colour a little modelling paste grey and make 2 teddies heads and 2 of each arm. Attach arms over tops of mitten and bootie. Attach heads. Brush teddies cheeks, inside ears and paws with pink powder. Dip a cocktail stick into black paste colour and mark eyes. Mix colour with a little water and paint noses. Colour a little sugarpaste grey and soften with water (p1). Place in a small piping bag and pipe over teddies spreading with a damp paintbrush, then dabbing the paintbrush to get the fur effect.

3 Shape small triangles of modelling paste for the hats. Mark creases where the hats bend with a dresden tool. Attach over sides of teddies heads. Attach a small white bobble and a trim. Dust hats with snowflake lustre.

4 Roll out white modelling paste and cut out snowflakes. Dust with snowflake lustre before attaching randomly over cake and one on each mitten.

# Rudolf and Friends!

20cm (8in) iced cake, 30.5cm (12in) cake drum, 225g sugarpaste, 225g marzipan, royal icing, Mexican paste, 3 pots of white magic sparkles ground finer (p1), edible glue (p1), isopropyl alcohol.

Paste Colour: Pink, paprika, egg yellow, dark brown (SF).

Powder Colours: Caramel, pink, white, black, red (SC), gold, snowflake lustre (SK).

Reindeer head mould (Karen Davies), small holly cutter from rocking horse set (PC), no.1 piping nozzle, 12mm double closed curve serrated crimper, pastry brush, a selection of painting and dusting brushes.

**1** Place cake on board. Cover board with sugarpaste. Emboss with the holly cutter. Dust with snowflake lustre. Mix isopropyl alcohol with gold powder and paint holly. Brush around bottom of cake with edible glue. Roll a long thin sausage of sugarpaste, attach around cake then crimp. Paint crimped edge gold.

**2** Colour some Mexican paste brown with paste colour. Roll pieces into small balls, then shape into teardrops. Treat the mould as a guide for size rather than a mould for the antlers. Check the size of the teardrops against the large antlers on the mould. Place a small and a large into each side of the shape. Remove then roll the two ends together. Leave to dry. You will need 18 – 20 pairs. When dry dust with brown powder.

**3** Colour marzipan with a little pink and paprika paste colour. Roll smooth balls then into ovals before pressing into the largest reindeer head. Remove from mould. Dust cheeks and inside ears pink. Dust around the face with brown but make the top of the face slightly darker. Paint the eyes white. Use black to paint the pupils looking left, right, up or down. Add a tiny white dot into the pupil. Paint the noses mostly black and a few red.

**4** Thin the glue with water if needed. You will need your glue to spread easily and not be too thick. Use a pastry brush to spread thinly and evenly over cake. Cover with magic sparkles.

**5** Attach reindeer heads randomly over cake with royal icing. Attach antlers. Colour a little royal icing yellow and pipe a name under each head. Paint lettering gold.

# Where's Rudolf?

25cm (10in) hexagonal cake (measured side to side) marzipanned, iced and placed on a 38cm (15in) iced cake drum, Mexican paste (p1), modelling paste (p1), a little royal icing, edible glue (p1), isopropyl alcohol, white magic sparkles (BK), cornflour, trex.

Paste Colour: : Red extra, spruce green, dark brown, egg yellow, Black, (SF).

Powder colours: Silver, brilliant gold, snowflake lustre (SK), red, snowflake, pink, black, brown (SC).

Reindeer head mould and bootie mould (Karen Davies), funky alphabet (FMM), Christmas tree cutter (large) from set of three (PME), bow cutter small (JEM), envelope cutter (JEM), size guide (CC), no.1 piping nozzle, non stick rolling pin and board, sponge pad, selection of paint and dusting brushes.

**1** Colour some Mexican paste red. Grease a non stick rolling out board with trex and roll out paste. Lightly grease cutters and cut out lettering. Leave to dry on a sponge pad. Dust with snowflake lustre.

**2** Colour a little mexican paste brown. Rub a little trex on to your fingers then roll 2 small balls of paste into thin teardrop shapes and lay into the small antlers on the mould. The antlers are more of a size and shape guide than an actual mould. Trim to fit, remove and roll the ends together. Make 6 sets of small antlers and 1 large. Leave to dry.

**3** Colour some mexican paste light brown. Roll long thin sausages and cut into 20, 2.5cm lengths. Press small balls of brown Mexican paste into the mould for the hooves. Release from mould and attach to ends of legs with edible glue. Leave to dry.

**4** Make 1 large reindeer head and 6 small. Lay on kitchen paper and dust brown powder colour around top half of head. Brush

pink powder onto cheeks and into ears. Brush a little glue onto end of antlers and push into heads. Leave to dry. Mix isopropyl alcohol with powder colour and paint noses and eyes.

**5** Use a large dusting brush to cover iced board with snowflake lustre. Soften some sugarpaste with water (p1) and place in a piping bag with a no.1 nozzle. Pipe a small plain shell around base of cake.

**6** Use glue to attach large head to centre of cake. Attach lettering starting from the centre of each word. Use a damp paintbrush and brush around reindeers head. Sprinkle with some magic sparkles.

**7** Colour some Mexican paste grey. Cut out the envelope. Put a little folded kitchen paper into the centre, then fold in sides. Brush edges with a little glue, then fold up the bottom piece. Leave to dry then brush with silver dust.

**8** Colour some Mexican paste green and cut out 4 trees. Cut 3 in half lengthways. Leave to dry. Dust with snowflake then attach whole tree to side of cake. Attach a centre half with green royal icing. Attach 2 pieces evenly into each side. Attach the 4 legs and then the head. Pipe some snow with royal icing onto the tree and add some magic sparkles. Grind remaining sparkles finer (p1) and set aside for later.

**9** Use the size guide to measure a size 15 ball of modelling paste. Colour brown. Roll into a ball and attach to side of cake. Paint different shades of brown dots all over to resemble a Christmas pudding. Brush ends of 4 legs with a little glue and push into ball. Soften a little royal icing, colour pale yellow and pipe over top for custard. Attach head.

**10** Colour some modelling paste red and use the mould to make a Christmas stocking. Press bow in and leave to dry. Attach a strip of white modelling paste around top of stocking. Brush thinly with glue and cover with magic sparkles.

**11** Colour a size 16 ball of modelling paste yellow. Shape into a square to resemble a present. Brush with gold powder. Roll out green mexican paste on a board greased with trex. Brush with snowflake lustre. Cut out narrow strips for ribbon to attach around the parcel. Cut out a bow and attach. Attach legs and head.

**12** Remove kitchen paper from envelope. Insert a small piece of brown paste into envelope for reindeer body. Attach legs and head using royal icing. Attach envelope to cake at a slight angle with royal icing.

**13** To make the snowball, roll a size 15 ball of modelling paste with trex on your hands. Roll into magic sparkles and attach to cake. Attach legs and head.

# Clown Birthday Cake

15cm (6in) cake marzipanned and iced in ivory sugarpaste, 28cm (11in) cake board, 350g ivory sugarpaste, modelling paste, Mexican paste, a little royal icing, edible glue (p1), isopropyl alcohol, trex.

Paste Colours: **Pink (SF).**

Powder Colours: **Lilac, pink, yellow, black, white, mint green (SC), snowflake lustre (SK).**

Spray Colour: **Pearl (PME).**

Clown mould (Karen Davies), flowers from fairy set (PC), blossom from confetti set (PC), no.42 piping nozzle, non stick rolling out board, sponge pad.

1   Grease a non stick board, the blossom and the flower cutters with trex. Roll out Mexican paste thinly. Do not lift and turn the paste as you roll. Cut out 5 blossoms and 8 of the flower groups from the fairy set. Re-grease the cutters between each use. Dust the flowers and leaves then finish with snowflake lustre. Leave to dry on a sponge pad.

2   Ice board and emboss with the blossom cutter. Dust blossoms lilac and pink. Give the pink blossoms a lilac centre and the lilac a pink. Spray iced board with pearl lustre. Place cake into centre of board. Place royal icing in a piping bag with a no.42 nozzle and pipe a small shell around base of cake. Leave to dry then dust with snowflake lustre.

3   Mix a little green powder with alcohol and paint some grass where clown will stand. Press modelling paste into mould and release. Check on the top of the cake where to pipe the lettering. Colour a little royal icing pink and pipe lettering.

4   Dust clowns cheeks then paint eyes with black powder mixed with isopropyl alcohol. Add a tiny white highlight to eyes. Paint nose and hair. Dust dress and hat, then paint small spots. When dry, dust over dress and hat with snowflake lustre. Attach to top of cake.

5   Paint a few background stems where flowers will be placed. Colour a little royal icing green and pipe a few stems from top and bottom of clown's hands. Attach blossoms. Pipe some royal icing around each corner, touching the cake board and the piping, then attach flowers.

# Puppy Birthday

23 x 18cm (9 x 7in) cake, 36 x 25.5cm (14 x 10in) cake board, 1.3kg (3lb) of sugarpaste, modelling paste, mexican paste, royal icing, hint of blue and white magic sparkles ground finer (p1), dark brown and light brown sugar, cornflour, edible glue, isopropyl alcohol, trex.

Paste Colours: **Spruce green, dark brown, ice blue (SF).**

Powder Colours: **Pink, gingho, marigold, cream, black, white (SC), snowflake lustre, silver, iris fairy dust (SK).**

Dog mould (Karen Davies), flower cutter from teddy bear picnic set (PC), funky alphabet (FMM), 2cm closed single curve serrated crimpers (PME), size guide (CC), new nailbrush, selection of paint / dusting brushes, no.1 & 2 piping nozzles, non stick rolling board, sponge pad.

1  Colour 1.1kg of sugarpaste green. Place cake on board and cover with sugarpaste. Press the nailbrush repeatedly into a 4cm strip along lower edge of top of cake. Crimp around top edge of cake. Ice board (4 strips may be used – grass effect will cover joins) then emboss with nailbrush. Crimp around edge of board. Dip a large dusting brush into water and squeeze out as much as possible. Brush over the grass on cake and board re-dampening when necessary. Sprinkle area with white sparkles. Soften a little green sugarpaste with water and place in a piping bag with a no.1 nozzle. Pipe a small plain shell around base of cake.

2  Colour some Mexican paste blue. Grease a rolling board and the required letters with trex. Roll out the Mexican paste thinly then cut out the letters. Remove paste from around the letters, then place letters on a sponge pad.

3  With modelling paste, use the dog mould to make 2 dogs and one head. Dust the tongues, inside the ears and under the paws with a little pink powder colour. Mix isopropyl alcohol with black powder colour and paint the noses and eyes. Paint a tiny white highlight into each eye.

4  Make 2 bones from the mould. Dust with a little cream powder colour. Shape a slightly bigger bone by hand and colour with iris powder.

5  Colour a little royal icing blue and place in a bag with a no.2 nozzle. Pipe the words 'Happy Birthday To' in the centre at the top of the cake. Brush the letters for the name thinly with glue. Cover with the blue sparkles. Attach to cake. Paint the piped words with snowflake lustre mixed with isopropyl alcohol. Attach one dog to the centre of the cake and one to its left.

6  Roll out white Mexican paste thinly on a board greased with trex. Grease the flower cutter with trex and cut out 7 flowers. Remove excess paste from board then dust with yellow, snowflake and green. Attach flowers to each bottom corner of cake and between the dogs.

7  Model the digging dog in white modelling paste. Use the size guide to measure the pieces of paste (p1). Shape a front paw from a size 6 ball of paste and the back paw from a size 7 (long teardrop shapes). Attach to cake at the same angle that the paw / leg will be over them. The body is a size 14 ball of paste flattened into an egg shape. Attach slightly over paws. Shape front leg from a size 9 and the back leg from a size 12. The tail is a size 5. Now attach the moulded head.

8  Soften some sugarpaste with water (p1). Colour some of it brown and place both softened pastes in piping bags. Pipe sections of the dogs and spread icing over with a damp paintbrush. Dab at the icing to give a fluffy effect. Attach bones to dogs as shown. Brush a little glue thinly under the digging dog then press some soft brown sugar into it.

9  Roll out a piece of Mexican paste thinly and cut a square 5 x 5cm. Dust with iris powder colour, scrunch up, then attach next to middle dog. Pipe a bow onto the wrapped bone and an undone bow onto the centre dog's wrapping paper.

10  Mix isopropyl alcohol with silver powder colour and paint paw prints around sides of cake. To do this, paint a small circle then 3 much smaller circles close together on edge of larger circle.

Happy Birthday To
SAM

20cm (8in) cake covered in pink or blue sugarpaste, 250g sugarpaste, modelling paste, 250g natural coloured marzipan, royal icing, 1 pot each of purple and hint of lilac magic sparkles (girl) or blue and hint of blue (boy) ground finer (p1), isopropyl alcohol, edible glue, trex.

Paste Colours: Paprika, pink, black, appropriate school uniform colour, grape violet (girl) ice blue (boy), egg yellow (only for blonde hair), dark brown (SF).

Powder Colours: Pink, white, black, brown, lilac, eye colour (SC), snowflake lustre, silver (SK).

Both cakes: Small face mould, baby and teddy mould (Karen Davies), no.1 & no.42 piping nozzles, stitch wheel / dresden tool (PME), funky alphabet set (FMM), embosser on board edge from set 3 border designs (HP), size guide (p1) (CC), a selection of dusting and paintbrushes, tape measure.

Girl's cake: Small bow cutters from make a cradle set or confetti set (PC), embosser for ballet dress from set 10 flower embroidery (HP), flower from confetti set (PC), small blossom from confetti set (PC), embosser on large girls dress teddy plaque (PC), garrett frill cutter, frilling / mouth tool (JEM)

Boy's cake: Small funky star (JEM), small star (PC), button embossing sticks (HP).

Both cakes:

1 Ice board and emboss around edge. Dust around the outside of the board with snowflake lustre. Place cake on board. Colour a little royal icing grey with the black paste colour and pipe a small plain shell around base of cake (for boys cake use a no.42 nozzle to pipe a small shell).

2 Colour marzipan to skin colour with a little pink and paprika. For a darker skin colour add dark brown to required shade. Make the 3 largest size faces using the face mould. Trim off the necks. Make the baby's head from the baby and teddy mould. Put tiny balls of marzipan into the hands of the baby mould. Measure a size 15 ball of paste using the size guide and colour lilac. Brush the thinnest amount of glue possible at back of hands. Reserve a little lilac paste for later then mould the baby's body. Emboss sleepsuit with the small blossom and dust lilac. Attach body to cake with glue.

3 Dust the cheeks of the 4 faces pink. Mix isopropyl alcohol with white powder and paint eyes (if you want the baby asleep do not paint yet). Mix colour for eyes and paint looking in directions required. Paint pupils in black then add a white highlight. Mix brown powder with water and use a very fine brush to paint eyebrows. Mix black with water and use the fine brush to paint a line across tops of eyes then eyelashes. For a sleeping baby, use either black or brown powder mixed with water to paint a fine line along bottom of the eye and a few eyelashes.

4 Colour some Mexican paste grey. Grease a rolling out board and the flower cutters with trex (stars instead of flowers for boy's cake). Cut out 14 large flowers for girl or 12 large stars for boy. Colour a little lilac or blue Mexican paste depending on girl/boy and cut out either 22 small blossoms or 22 small stars. Brush flowers / large stars with silver powder. Paint centre of blossoms silver. Brush blossoms / small stars with glue and cover with the lighter magic sparkles. Colour a little Mexican paste Purple / dark blue and cut out '21'. Brush thinly with glue and cover with magic sparkles.

5 Place largest head in position on cake. Mark where feet will be at bottom of cake. Use a tape measure to mark half way between top of head and feet to mark position for waist. Lay the 2 other size heads on cake positioning evenly. Measure half way again from top of head to feet position to mark waist. Remove larger three heads from cake.

Girl's cake:

1 For the eldest girls legs, use the size guide to measure a size 13 ball of marzipan. Divide in half and make a leg with each half. shape and attach. Mark toes with a knife. Attach a small flattened ball of lilac modelling paste under the foot. Attach a strip of lilac paste across top of foot. Dust with snowflake lustre. Use a size 13 ball of marzipan for body. Shape the waist, then a chest and finally pinch out a neck. Attach to cake.

2 Colour some modelling paste grey – or appropriate colour. Roll out thinly on trex and cut an oblong that would cover the body. Place over body or use a tape measure to see where to trim. Use round cutters such as piping nozzle tops to shape for arms and neck. Emboss a pattern and use a stitch wheel to mark hem and neck. Brush dress with silver powder. Attach to body with glue. Dress can be gathered in t waist and a belt attached. Make a small bag with a wedge of lilac paste. Brush with glue and cover with sparkles. Attach to dress. Attach a thin grey sausage of modelling paste to top and 2 small teardrop shapes for fastener. Each arm is a size 10 on the size guide. Roll a sausage, thinning towards wrist and flattening for hand. Cut a 'v' out to get the thumb then mark fingers with a knife. Attach arms. Paint ends of fingers and toes pink. Attach head.

3 Pipe lettering using a no.1 nozzle and grey royal icing. Mix isopropyl alcohol and silver powder to paint top of bag, lettering and border around bottom of cake. Attach the '21' but check the postion the 2 middle heads will be first.

CONTINUED...

Where have the years gone?

Becky is **21**

**4** Ballerina's legs are each a size 10. Pinch out a little on one to the left and one to the right. Attach to cake and attach a ballet shoe to each. Roll out some modelling paste thinly and cut out strips for ribbon. Dust strips and shoes with snowflake lustre, then attach strips around legs. Roll out modelling paste on a board dusted with icing sugar. Cut out a garrett frill. Cut open then trim a piece 7 scallops in length. Frill with the frilling tool, dust with snowflake lustre and attach just over half way up legs. Repeat adding until you have approximately 8 layers of frills, increasing the length as necessary to get the tutu shape.

**5** Shape a size 11 piece of paste for top of dress. Attach to cake and emboss with the flower. Dust with snowflake. Shape top of chest and neck from a size 7 piece of marzipan and arms each from a size 8. Attach to top of dress then attach 2 straps. Make a tiny rose bud for each strap by flattening a thin sausage of paste and rolling up tightly. Attach to straps then dust with snowflake. Attach head.

**6** The school girls legs are a size 7. Attach to cake then cover ankles with white socks and add balls of grey paste for shoes. Add a skirt and mark pleats with a dresden tool. Make a school book from an oblong of white sugarpaste. Mark pages with a knife then attach a cover made from modelling paste. Paint ABC on front cover. Add a body in the required colour from a size 11 piece of modelling paste. Mark hem of jumper with a dresden tool. Attach book. Shape hands from a size 6 ball of marzipan cut in half, cut thumbs and mark fingers. Shape each sleeve from a size 8. Bend and mark at elbow, make a hole to insert hand, then mark sleeve cuff with the dresden tool. Attach to body. Add a small white collar and attach head.

**7** Colour a little royal icing for hair. Add a little brown to yellow for blonde hair. Place in a bag with a no.42 nozzle. Pipe appropriate hairstyle on each figure adding bows required. For the baby, spread a little royal icing on to head then dab with a paintbrush.

**8** Attach flowers and blossoms randomly around cake sides and a few on top.

Boy's cake:

**1** From a size 16 ball of blue modelling paste, roll a sausage, flatten slightly, cut in half to separate legs, then shape for jeans. Mark hems and seams with a stitch wheel and dresden tool. Dust seams, hems etc with dark blue powder. Attach to cake and add balls of grey paste for shoes. Shape a body from a size 13 ball of marzipan, pulling up a neck. Roll out white modelling paste and cut an oblong for shirt. Check it for size and trim to fit cutting a small v at the bottom and a larger v at the top. Mark a hem with the stitch wheel. Attach to body then add a strip of white paste up the front. Mark with the stitch wheel. Attach small balls of paste and emboss with the button sticks.

**2** Colour a little marzipan brown and shape a beer bottle. Attach a label and paint the word beer by mixing black powder colour with alcohol. Attach beer to body. Roll 2 sausages of white paste each from a size 11 and shape for sleeves. Make a hole at wrist for hand. Shape hands each from a size 7 ball of paste. Flatten a teardrop shape, cut fingers with scissors then push the point up the sleeve. Mark elbow creases with the dresden tool and attach to body placing hands over beer. Cut out cuffs, mark with the stitch wheel and attach over sleeves. Cut out 2 collar pieces, mark with the stitch wheel and attach either side of neck. Attach head.

**3** Pipe lettering using a no.1 nozzle and grey royal icing. Mix isopropyl alcohol and silver powder to paint top of bag, lettering and border around bottom of cake. Attach the '21' but check the postion the 2 middle heads will be first.

**4** Roll 2 sausages of marzipan each from a size 10. Attach to cake but bend one leg and mark with the dresden tool. Cover lower legs with coloured paste and mark with the dresden tool. Shape boots from balls of black paste. Add tiny balls of paste to sole for studs. Add white strips over top. Cut out an oblong of white paste measuring 7 x 4cm. Cut a v out of the bottom of the shorts and gather up the top. Attach over legs. Attach a half ball of paste under the foot and paint to resemble a football. From a size 12 piece of marzipan shape a flattened teardrop for the body and attach. Cover with a coloured piece of paste for the shirt body having cut out a v for the neck first. Mark hem with the stitch wheel. Arms are each shaped from a size 9 as before and hands are a size 7 divided in half. Attach arms, hands and head.

**5** Shape a pair of trousers from a size 13 ball of paste and attach. Add small balls of paste for shoes. The jumper body is a size 11 and the arms each size 8, the hands a size 6 cut in half. Make book as for girl and attach to body, placing hands over. Attach head.

**6** Colour a little royal icing for hair. Place in a piping bag, then pipe on hair using a damp paintbrush to spread and make hairstyle.

**7** Attach large and small stars randomly around cake sides and a few on top

# One Tier Wedding Cake

25 x 20cm (10 x 8in) iced cake placed on a 35 x 30cm (14 x 12in) cake drum, 400g sugarpaste, Mexican paste, 90g Marzipan, royal icing, modelling paste, edible glue, isopropyl alcohol, trex.

**Paste Colours:** Ice blue, grape violet, pink, paprika, hair colours – egg yellow, dark brown (SF).

**Powder Colours:** Silver, snowflake (SK), brown, black, white, pink, lilac, blue, green (SC).

**Spray Colour:** Baby blue (PME).

Large face mould (Karen Davies), lace Strip cutter (PC), small horse shoe cutter (PC), no.42 & no.1 piping nozzles, small daisy/marguerite plunger cutter (PME), raw silk rolling pin (HP), selection of painting / dusting brushes, a piece of soft sponge, non stick rolling board.

**1** Ice cake board and emboss a pair of horse shoes in each corner. Mix isopropyl alcohol with silver powder colour and paint.

**2** Roll out Mexican paste thinly and cut out an oblong 15 x 11cm. Cut out 2 strips measuring 15 x 1.5cm and 2 measuring 11 x 1.5cm. Make sure all pieces are straight and leave to dry.

**3** Grease a non stick board and the lace cutter with trex. Roll out Mexican paste thinly – do not lift paste, then cut out 2 pieces 18cm long and 2 pieces 14cm long (move cutter along to get a strip long enough but do not press too hard where you join up pattern). On one edge of each piece, mark 2cm along from each end. Trim with a knife from these points diagonally to end of strip on opposite side. Check corners will sit neatly together when joined for picture frame. Leave to dry.

**4** Colour 3 pieces of Mexican paste pink, blue and lilac. Roll out on a little icing sugar. Brush with snowflake lustre and cut out approximately 30 daisies in each colour. As you cut each daisy out, press the plunger down while on a hard surface to emboss the pattern, then push the flower out into soft sponge to shape. Leave to dry. Grease a non stick board and the horse shoe cutter with trex and roll out Mexican paste. Cut out 2 horse shoes.

**5** Spray the oblong of white Mexican paste with a little blue for a sky background. Attach to centre of cake with royal icing. Mix alcohol with powder colours and paint lace frame. Paint the strips of white Mexican paste and the horse shoes silver. Using a no.1 nozzle, pipe the lettering onto the cake in royal icing. Leave to dry then paint silver.

**6** Divide marzipan in half and roll each piece smooth. Press each piece into the face mould and remove. Rub pink powder colour well into a dusting brush and dust cheeks. Paint white into eyes, then the colour so they will be looking towards each other. Paint in the pupils then a tiny white highlight (a lustre powder can be brushed above the brides eyes as eyeshadow). Use a fine paintbrush to paint the eyebrows and eyelashes but this time, mix the colour with water. Attach grooms head to the background piece using royal icing, leaving a little space for the shoulders. Colour a little modelling paste

dark grey for the grooms shoulders, a colour for his tie and a small piece green. Keep a little grey for the lapels then shape and attach shoulders underneath the neck. Add a small white triangle, then shape and attach a tie. Add a white collar then roll out a strip of coloured paste and cut two lapels. Attach then shape a leaf from the green paste and attach with a flower. Make sure the flower is not too high for when the frame is attached later (trim edge of groom to the background if needed).

**7** Roll out a piece of modelling paste thinly on a little trex. Cut a piece measuring 10cm square. Use the silk rolling pin across the paste, then dust with snowflake lustre. Turn over and turn back a narrow hem down the sides of the veil. Gather together at the top then roll the gathers to flatten. Attach next to groom and flatten the area the brides head will cover. Attach brides head then trim veil so it does not run over the background edge. Shape some marzipan for the brides shoulders. Attach joining neatly to the neck. Place a little royal icing in a piping bag and pipe a small row of pearls over join. Leave to dry then paint with snowflake lustre.

**8** Colour some royal icing for the hair. Pipe grooms hair first then the bride using the no.42 nozzle. Add a few flowers and leaves into the brides hair for her headdress.

**9** Attach silver strips upright around edge of background using royal icing. Leave to dry. Pipe royal icing along top edge of each strip then attach lace frame pieces.

**10** Attach daisies around bottom of cake with royal icing. Attach horse shoes to frame and one of each colour flower. Paint all flower centres silver.

Congratulations

Dave & Sue

# Face Moulds

Many people say that when modelling, their faces let them down. I have tried to help with this by bringing out moulds for faces that have been made from hand modelled sugar figures. The moulds are deliberately simple so that it is easy for the cake decorator to adapt to the face / character desired. At the moment, we have 7 sizes, the small mould has 5 faces measuring 17mm, 24mm, 29mm, 34mm and 40mm, the medium is 50mm and the large 62mm. You are able to produce a head flat at the back to lay on top of a cake, or the whole head for stand up figures. You will see that it is possible from one face to produce any character: young, old, male or female. As you look through this book, every face has different characteristics – all depending on what has been done to the basic face. I like to use marzipan for any skin parts on models and it works perfectly with the mould. Modelling paste is also ideal. Whichever paste you use, colour with a little paprika (peach) and pink for skin colour. For a darker skin colour I like to start with the basic skin colour, then add brown until the desired colour is reached.

1. This picture shows the heads as they come out of the mould. First the flat, then the full head. When the full head is moulded, roll a ball and lay it in the mould to check the size. Roll the paste very smooth then make a point to aim at the nose in the mould before pressing it in. For the full head, you should keep the paste fuller at the top of the head, sloping down narrower into the neck. Push the paste away from the edge of the mould to prevent a deep ridge forming. To get the paste into the ears, push paste between two fingers then press into ears. Turn the mould over and flex gently to release the head. Keep it close to the worktop as it may fall out quite easily. Gently rub to smooth the ridge to remove as much as possible. If the head will have hair this does not matter so much. If you have too much paste around the ears or where the neck joins the head, a dresden tool or a knife can be used to tidy.

3. Dust cheeks with a little pink powder colour. Use a large brush and rub the colour well into kitchen paper making sure there is no loose powder on your brush before applying.

2. Now you can alter the features. Press the ears back or push in if hair is to be piped over. A singing mouth can be made with a paintbrush handle. For an older person, add cheeks with a mouth tool and lines with a Dresden tool.

4. Mix isopropyl alcohol with powder colour to paint whites of eyes. They can be half painted for an elderly or sleepy person (see picture 9). For a sleeping face, mix brown powder colour with water and using a fine paintbrush, paint a line underneath the eye and a few eyelashes.

5 Paint in the eye colour. You can just paint black if you wish. Always paint the eye looking up or down, left or right — never in the middle unless you want a startled look!

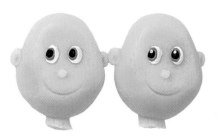

6 Paint in the pupil. Finally, paint a small white highlight into the eye and see what a difference that makes.

7 Because the eyes on the faces protrude slightly it is easy to paint a fine line across the top of the eye (or under). When painting eyelashes and eyebrows use colour mixed with water and a fine brush.

8 Hair can be piped on with either royal icing or softened sugarpaste. You could also use pieces of sugarpaste marked with a knife or a claygun.

9 This picture shows a baby's face and an old man's face — both from the same mould.

# The Hairy Bakers..!

In July 2008 I made a cake topper of a Volkswagen camper van for the BBC2 programme 'The Hairy Bakers' starring Si King and Dave Myers. When they came to pick up the cake top, I presented them with this cake of themselves.

They had been on a cake decorating course to make the wedding cake in the programme, so I had made the cake showing them doing this. I had made the faces on the figures using my medium size head moulds. This shows how the faces from the moulds can be adapted to look like anyone!

# Using the Moulds

1 Always wash and thoroughly dry new moulds before use.

2 Dust preferably with cornflour. It can be placed in a piece of disposable cleaning cloth, a dishcloth, a popsock, a nappy liner and tied at the top. After dusting mould, turn over and tap out excess. Icing sugar can also be used.

3 Both modelling paste and marzipan work well in the moulds. Always use natural coloured marzipan. If marzipan is a little soft, Tylo (CMC) powder can be added to bring to the correct consistency. Sugarpaste can work in the flatter moulds such as the mitten and bootie.

4 Modelling paste is usually half flower paste half sugarpaste, but different makes can have different effects so you may need to alter the proportions. The paste should be soft enough to show the detail from the mould but not so soft that it distorts as it is removed.

5 The paste should always be level with the back of the mould before removing. If you have too much, trim some off, remove from mould and start again. If you leave in the mould to trim, the paste may move slightly giving double impressions.

6 Before pressing your paste into the mould, make sure the surface area is smooth and keep any creases to the back. It helps to have the paste a similar shape to the mould before pressing in. Do not place a round ball in. Dust your fingers with cornflour or icing sugar before pressing the paste. This prevents it lifting and moving giving double imprints. To get the paste into small areas such as ears, push paste between two fingers so it comes up between them then push down into ear etc.

7 To remove from the mould, turn the mould over and flex slightly.

8 Coloured paste can be used or the finished figures can be dusted or painted. To paint mix isopropyl alcohol with powder colours for best results. With figures such as the teddy bear, you can also put a different colour into paws and ears etc then brush thinly with a little glue and put the main colour on top.

9 With the baby and teddy mould you can mould the head, hands and body separately with the different coloured pastes required then join together on the cake. This can be useful for beginners with little experience of using moulds.

10 Moulded figures can be adapted to many different designs from the basic figure i.e. softened sugarpaste (p1) can be brushed on to animals for a fur effect.

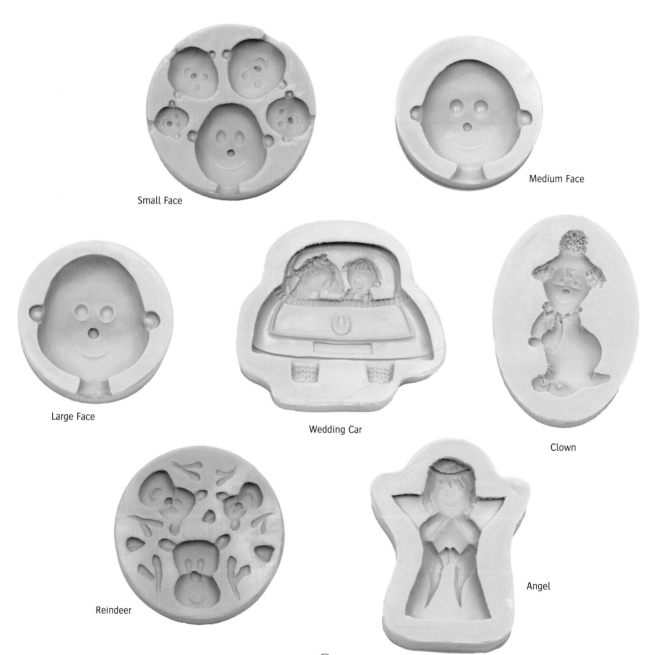

Small Face

Medium Face

Large Face

Wedding Car

Clown

Reindeer

Angel

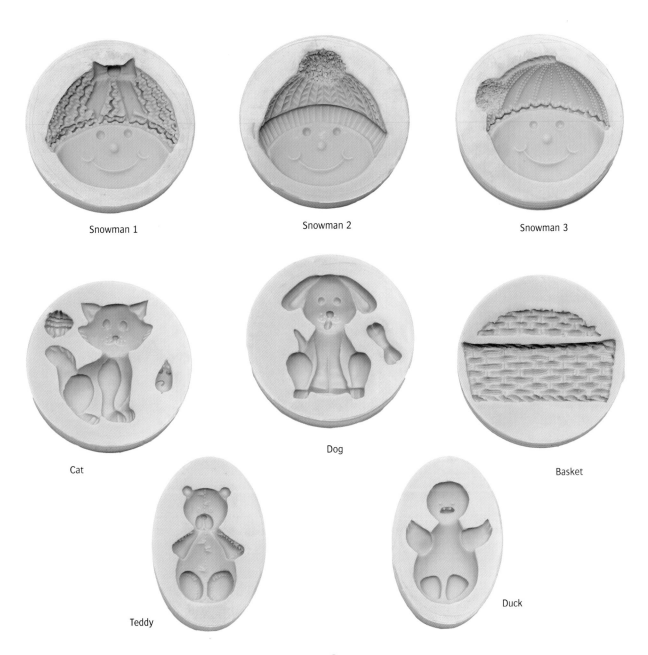

Snowman 1

Snowman 2

Snowman 3

Cat

Dog

Basket

Teddy

Duck

Nursery Border

Rabbit

Baby and Teddy

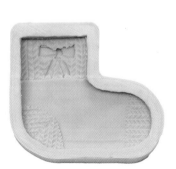

Bootie

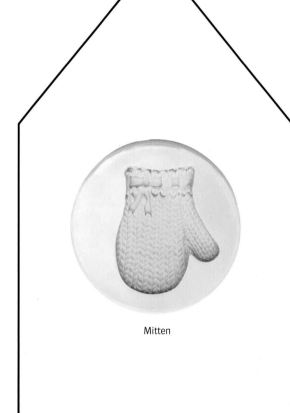

Mitten

Cot Pattern: Sleeping Baby, Pages 10-11